END CEREMONIES

C000157685

Stuart McPherson is a prize-winning poet from the UK. Recent poems have appeared in *Butcher's Dog Magazine*, *Bath Magg*, *Poetry Wales*, *Anthropocene* and *Blackbox Manifold*. His debut micro pamphlet *Pale Mnemonic* was published in April 2021 by Legitimate Snack. His pamphlet *Waterbearer* was published in December 2021 by Broken Sleep Books. A debut full length collection *Obligate Carnivore* was published by Broken Sleep Books in August 2022. In October 2022, Stuart was the winner of the Ambit Annual Poetry Competition.

End Ceremonies

Stuart McPherson

Broken Sleep Books

ISBN: 978-1-915760-32-6 (Paperback)
ISBN: 978-1-915760-68-5 (Hardback)

Cover designed by Aaron Kent & Joe Kent

Edited & Typeset by Aaron Kent

Broken Sleep Books Ltd
Rhydwen
Talgarreg
Ceredigion
SA44 4HB

Broken Sleep Books Ltd
Fair View
St Georges Road
Cornwall
PL26 7YH

For Caroline & Dorrie

Contents

IV

V

VI

VII

You can't look at yourself in the ocean.
Your looks fall apart like tendrils of light
— Frederico García Lorca

I

Gradualism

And I wonder just how long
it might take for us to liquify.
Our home, our hearts. Strength

of written oath once witnessed.
Nothing stays the same forever.
Not the crumbling of brick, not

the cleanliness of air. Tinnitus of
running horse, the blacksmith in
our ears. A colossal folding up of

night. Its charcoal non-existence.
There is comfort to it, *this absolute
knowing.* Such tiny shoes behind

a door. The colour of past efforts
outgrown. Two red flares sat idly
scattered right beside an open gate.

Gasp Reflex

You and I, the same shape.
Same curve of spine, same
tone of black sympathetic

pupil depth. A question of
practicing cold-water shock
response. Synchronicities of

sharpest breath. Vain hope,
that when your iris fills with
salt, when you hold yourself

tight around the knees, that
you would know not to feel
the weight of ripping tides.

My shame pulls down upon
young legs, beneath thickest
ocean; vast mercurial bodies.

Slabbed & leaden, born from
breach. Locked within rifts of
failure re-written & disguised.

Its tentacles around your waist,
afar, asunder, abrasive seabed.
An infinitude of Octopus eyes.

In Time I'll Fade Away

i

Mount Jupiter or thrown
shadow. Mist as sentinel haunting
guillotined sun equivalence.

Young cub. Eight feet in unison upon
the ferns; dewy, orbed. Upon my torso
painted north east; *written word of compass.*

This musk of soil beneath stomach's matted
fur, this lament of earth. *Little woodland runner,*
keen as hawk, soft as tears, *keep close to me.*

ii

Raspberries; hazelnuts in Autumn.
An anxiousness of chocolate. Nothing
changes, *I still eat at night.*

Fascinate on the berries of an
English yew, the sorrow of broken
promises hung around your neck.

To reach inside my chest, investigate
the strength of walls; of moonlight reparation,
the cacao, the dance of end ceremonies.

Watch you grow strong bathing
in the ice melt, hanging upside-
down from the trunk.

Pride lumps in
the river of
my throat.

iii

Snapped branch; silver muzzle. Fill nostrils with
the blackness of powder as flesh is zippered
open. *Run far away.*

Rounding teeth, one-ton eight feet tall.
Explore ribcage from back to front, redeem
punctured neck vein affluence.

Emulsified; our blood as oil.
Stood upright to crush death's head.
The orbit wield of a hunters sword.

iv

Oranges, reds; Heron on the bank.
A concertina of silk folded into
wooden baskets.

Pine scented. Eyelashes stood
upright with migrating birds,
your face; its gentleness.

Story written as scar, healed as
vow ascending skin. A thistle seed
guided through air.

Within sadness.
Eternal love.
Or both.

First Born

To you, there is a corridor.
A pushing up of fists into throats or a
sharp apple rolled beneath light.

To settle against my feet. *Be swallowed.*
You're not there yet, but a new father
splitting at the seams. A mother's

ghost idling below hands, time anything
other than a sweeping brush. To the
knives, there is lustre.

A readying for skin that once dreamt
about miracle births, the sucking hollow-
ness of a black tooth.

A wound or a grey slab chiselled & blown.
Sat beneath them all, this long luminescence,
is a heart, is a bird clipping its wings.

Alone. Waiting for your screams to come
swinging through the door, & deathless.
As alive as the first time we ever met.

The Heart Pushes Out, The Heart Rests

Every bloodied nose
    assessed in relation to
anatomies of the skull. Clothes
        filled out unbeknownst to time or
the graduations of a belt notch. *Sleep*
suppressant. Vested interests in the grey
    shades of skin, blood moon held
beneath eyelid. There are two of us
        here, you have spoken to us both.
We lied, the same as the chocolate and
        damson lied to your tongue. It isn't
difficult to split into two when partitioned by
    glass. We, and by that I mean us, deny all
in the same way a river denies the weight of
        a dying salmon. To float down
    rapids as two separate pieces of a
knotted branch. *The bears are on their haunches.*
    The ovaries, full of roe, ripe for the pawing.
Laid bare on the rocks, your mouth stained with
        Auburn is fear. *This is our ceremony.*
    Pressure is an ending, a snake's tongue.
Choose between starvation or rebirth into an
        estuary mouth. Water once known as cloud,
            once seen stabbed upon the knife of a
    mountaintop. Deliver me from trances, from
        tricks of the light. Scare me towards the
                fate of a dead man gasping his
                way back to life.

A Ribbon, Prior To Cutting

Taut tongue railing against a languorous breeze, rests
upon a scissor blade. Marled twisted innards, inward

facing. Candy pattern to gather up peppery shroud of
flies. Stretched out for long miles across memories of

hazy towns, sweet lullabies from a mother's mouth as
soft hair so gently stroked. Across the watercolours of

a trickling brook sat sunken into, sat swallowing over
new-born thighs tied around *that neck of his*. Rising up

and away, a drying up of holy waters. A red ribboning
around my waist, my jaw, unable to speak of blighted

lakes, jagged spire of drowned village church asked to
reappear from beneath its glossy sheet. A ceremonious

marriage. Of me to a sickened horse nudging apart the
last fruit of Autumn. This silence; my daughter's voice

encased in alloy. I am a shunted stubborn ship forward
bound, deafened by the scraping, a rusty blunted steel.

Cut. Falling open like sash curtains, like silk giving way.
A procession escaped, of rioting in the midnight streets.

Legion

Dragging inward the dead year's animal carcass. Its wavering spirit absorbent of all bad light, sucks cigarettes through cloth, an abrupt yellow belch. Anemone stood on iron hilltop, as silhouette. A flowerless mound of blood orange rust reaching for alignment, *north node in Taurus, Mars in Gemini.* Hold wilted bloom, the rotting marrow of a bruised stem. *Beautiful music grips the throat.* Whip of solar flare, red rope threaded through needle, the irreverence of a peacock tail. *Explode outwards.* Become nothing but the thinness of sugar. There are spiders in the luscious blueness of the strawberry thief. Last year's calendar, or the next. When will it stop or begin again? *neither really matter*, not the scratching in the roof, nor the redness beneath the stomach soaking into tissue like a kidney. *An ingrown hair.* The winter shrieks from its frozen grass. The gnawed swings in the park are moving, yet remain untouched.

Somnambulist

Feeling our limp hearts beat horizontally.
  Thinking of all the beautifully quiet rooms.
    Spears of light discarded, bent crudely into

lonely corners. From cars travelling without
  consent of roads. Deep blue rivers holding up
    bloated pale bodies. A headache, or heavy

dense pillow. It's believed that for every inch
  of sleep a record must be notched into walls,
    and there is something about the sadness

of headlamps, the solitude of one's own shape.
  Impossible to be captured *with accuracy,* but
    perhaps within our quiet whispers dropped

inside the depths of mattresses. Where ageing
  blood thickens to a slow shuffle, where creaks
    in floorboards exude every single fattened

footstep. A dancing of coded messages; *escape.*
  Your own name shouted from chalk outlines.
    The bodies peculiar disappearing act under

finely powdered lime and sand cement. *If only
you would listen,* like you did when you were so
    utterly certain that it was time for you to go.

Aubade For Daily Necrosis

With every opportune night, a
saddle. A chance to sit upon its
sumptuous cloak; *anonymised, deep*.
Risen up in the throat of each rotten
neck of year, the repetition of failing
time. In its hands, balled as fetus, a
dream of riding. To a swarming pool
of stars gliding across fingertips,
pouring through the curves; *iced
water*. All I ever wanted was to feel
the edges of a rooftop as I float away.
Taste the turquoise orange of every
stolen winter afternoon. Be free from
corrugation, the misery of the trees. If
you've been raised inside the carcass
of a horse, you'll know the smell of
marrow, of ribs. That desire is
anticipation, the bend of bone before
the break. I want to learn the spells of
quiet sleep, bewitch the daylight
hours with the plucked feather of a
hawk. We beg to share in morning
reveries; sit in silence. *No-one asked for
this*, to wipe away the iron richness,
an egregious violence of swollen lips.

Refuse / Fresh Fruit

Maybe we have always known.
Too afraid to tell or describe in
depth this gradual transparence.

Soaking in its patch away from sound.
Circle of sky hung up; end of grey
barrel. Magnolia plate settling in its sight.

Trigger happy for slow metal pushing
past unhampered flesh, ceilings pressed
upon flight. Slurp from shattered

mass, a sweetened mouth. Seeds between
piano teeth. Discarded, a rocking chair of
crescent skin. Worked by tool. *Deep furrowed.*

A see-saw apprehensive for the bag along
with all those awkward memories quietly
waiting to begin again.

Daytime Anxiety Practice

Shooting arm pain to sharpen such quick inward breaths. A half minded rattling incompatible with the *dressage* of a horse. Pirouetting on the blood of frost-bitten toes, swirl lavish arcs, concentric circles mapped as severance. *Daytime* is a strangled epiglottis choked on the steps of a lost Waltz. Our reluctance to move with any purpose. Good health or incantations of *how to really live.* Know that three four rhythm is a pig-eared rudiment failure, a polyglot heart squeezing out the oil of rotten language. This quickstep façade; a boat deck full of flat horizons ready to sail on salt foam seas. Maritime grief is a pouring out of oceans, of boat shaped tears. *Everyday hypochondria* as unregulated medical practice. Iron nails hit home with iron hammer. Motivational quotes are scoured beneath birdwing in terrible fonts. The fluorescent eyes of every black cat are tenterhooked in the zero hour.

Where Will I Be Kept When All of My Anger Has Disappeared?

An attic space to live in, hollow wasp.
Dancing between webs from wall-to-wall.
Settle lonely in your paper cone.

A homelessness of things now unable to fit.
Nauseous vampire, plushie wolf pup, you've lost
your methodologies. All that remains of this

room, a rhomboid. A sharp knife of light.
Old newspapers stained with sipping tea are
stacked by the breast.

A regurgitating up of. *Old headlines. Moral panic.*
A bitter inks outraged typeface. Outside, the
world can be seen as living and breathing.

The rise and fall of a button beautifully carved
and sailing in its royal night. Ivory peaks.
Lakes dust-dry, lapping at the lip.

Everything can be cleaned, and still, we all
suffer *somewhere*. I have a hunch. *Look upwards.*
A curious paleness presses at the gap.

Self-Transformation Mood Board

This centrality of question, of lineage. The gathering up of broken boughs ill- fated to a crudeness of rooted things. Memories cradled in the air, how softly plucked to fall and gathered. Placed by the tall trunk, our sequestered young mulch.

Albeit lacquer-less handles. An absent rake clatters to the floor asking to be gripped. There are pieces I have taken. Pieces picked up and mounted in place. Renovation tutorials that I have read and re-read. Misunderstandings gently removed with a low, blue heat.

Rubbing alcohol removes lips, clicks into place a droll mouth. Clicks together two white plates of a skull that used to let out deciduous leaves, a dusking light. A pink knife handle. Unironic right angle stabbed into the fat of it, the dry aged flesh.

Embedded as past history spatters in the hot oil of it's ludicrous self. *I pull out the blade.* Fill a plate with lusciousness. With the greenery of the fields, golden corn peeled open, its buttery sunlit kernels. I open my mouth to taste.

Eternally tied to the geometrics of the mind. Imprisoned spaces peered into, to gaze at hollow sockets supremely scaffolded. My own engineering from chin to ear to cranium, pulling at the clasp.

And cut wide open, reveals my habit for collecting teeth. I put a finger inside a dry socket just to smell its stink. My body or a dogs as it runs towards this open hand. A red mouth grinning with rescinded fangs before I grab the jaw just beneath.

Withdraw its skeleton from within, and from the pile make a pelt. Drape the bloody gown of skin around my shoulders. I howl as I step outside the ghost of my own shape, a worn wolfs head spitting into mirrors once resigned.

For this is all there is and can ever be. I have slept between the ribs of a deer. Felt its arrows from the outside in. *I will never be young again.* Repeat that to yourself, and in the fullest of moons ask- *But what might I become? What I am I now becoming?*

Signposts at the End of the World

absolutes | as in *existence* | as in *existing* | as in fragile
      beams in withered cavity of roof | to be killed during
sleep | as in redundancy memos | the compulsory failure
      of electric appliances | as in broken boilers | as in

performance reviews | as in agreeing to see sustained
      improvement | *yes- I'll do better* | *of course this matters*
more to me than the failing health of friends | *or walking*
      naked in the snow | as in to attach oneself to the Earth

as in *lock and load!* | as in every male boss I ever had has
      sounded like my father | as in how shrivelled my
manhood | not through poor pay | or lack of sex due to
      political states | but being trapped in the hidden

wormeries of aesthetic gardens | as in wanting nuclear war
      waiting for it all to end | anything to help liquify the
body |or forge new physical and mental propositions | as in
      self-sabotage | as in none of this is real | as in building

immolation cages to climb into | not to burn | but for others
      to see and possibly ask helpful questions | as in list
comprehensive detail | some presuppositions for happiness
      so that in the end ceremony | you can dance your

righteous dance | wear the right attire | as in everyone else
      knows better than you | as in *if you don't take care of*
yourself you don't love me | as in still treat yourself from time to
      time | as in those months you used the credit card to

take out cash | paid the minimum less interest | as in *don't tell*
      anyone | as in understand the meaning of vocation | as in
check your own blood pressure | wrestle with minutes and
      seconds knowing each suicide of space | meaning that

time eventually *end*s | we should socialise weekly with close
      friends | as in *if only I made you happy* | as in the extreme
guilt of fatherhood | aka *what I have inflicted on all of us* | as in
      I promise I won't buy anything online | as in tomorrow

book a lane to swim at slow to moderate pace | as in news
      reports of large hulks of space rock hurtling towards us all |
as in what we *should* have done | is *gone out* more often
      to eat | drink more Margaritas | than we ever did before

Half Life, Contradistinguished

Looking closely for mind and body connection amongst *all this positive change*, and perched, like a Goldcrest. This smallest bird unable to be caught sat chirping out its worry songs. I search in bakeries for soft bread, to ball up, throw overarm. Plaster it against the brickwork of a midnight pottery. *Masticated. Glazed.* Pieces of a boy, or once the memory of. These forward steps so remarkable. These *lamentations*. How to live within an ageing cast. This plaster of Paris cracked open to reveal fingers, thumbs, a voice. Yet despite the composition of sound and language, something pushes in the calories. Slopes downwards, a thick liquid to coat, spill over. It pools within the jaws of this pythonic existence, slips away like precious air. The way I finish your words, pinch at the neck your love, your care. My devotion is unquestionable, yet relentless tending to this grassy plot. The chiseling hammer round edged and hit plum centre; *ye olde English.* In half- life, to decay, shed this skin. Become cold with the naked curves of a torso. To *rise up* desolate phoenix, fly swiftly towards the setting sun.

II

All My Friends Are Getting Sick

Resisting arrest within six-sided
    isolation channels neatly stacked.

All flesh is woodworked; index finger
    to thumb pinched in gluey press

Blister pack resentment, as gospel song,
    as holy hands conjure *heavy touch.*

Our future a knuckling of ice soaked
    deep blue. Y*oung resignation animal.*

Under bloody bones, a snuffing out of
    moons terse light. Thirteen orbits or

thirteen chances for redemption sniffed
    as clots into cavity. *Volcanic black blood.*

Wilful ignorance is a vile split tongue.
    The analogue voice of a talking clock.

All I Hold, I Become

Inconvenient body
unpinned, resting in
palms small tortoise-
shell. Wind runner
raises up featherbeds.
Night handkerchief,
blood red stuffed into
bone holes. Magic trick,
a beak or the gradient
of forceps forced open,
closed, the heart beats,
fragile house, grenade
threat event, exploded.
Water *and* sustenance.
Aeration. Brittle teeth.
Ivory darts, a grievous
panacea. The smallest
of breaths. My full cup
poureth over. Crouch
concern bent double by
windowsills bowlegged.
Inflight, haphazard and
ungrateful. Lingering, a
cat dipped at both ends.
Questions etched, such
odd shapes in the rain.

From Memory to Real Life, Young Ghost

Eventual sleep holds its
backhand to the light. Cradles
joining skin between evening
zoetropes, retreats sepia fingers.
Scoured outlines arachnid
black. *Twelve silver lanterns.*
A silhouette of spider crab.
The night keeping score, river
water reflects knot-tied hook-
lengths. A bucket of writhing
eels full stomached. Endless
summer gorged on Perseids.
Shadow cracked Chinese bridge
as humid horse fields by the
banked edge empties of its flies.
Tangential body. Overflowing pool
anointed. *We met.* Talked excitedly
of possibilities, your changing shape.
Of how to make appointments.
Of how to speak with you
so quietly again.

Fuel for the Confession Fire

When they appear, hold moments of nostalgia deep in the
body. They rise up from thick wings beating on the Earth.

Daydreams are both a curse and a blessing. Freedoms of the
   spirit or a caged vulture feeding on our dark, exposed livers.

Of sight beyond the haze of pollen, dandelion seedheads
   travelling southwards towards an endless summer. It is

everything about death and dying that sits within regret, sits
   within cupped hands needing to be held. I see the first

   snow-caps. The frigid standpipe spitting at the sun. This
vision is a birthing, of *runt litters, the hungry.* The undeniable

   power held within the stomach of a young ghost. The radio
at night above my grandfather's bed. A Halloween moon

   worshipped behind the twitched curtain of a hollow house
freed from daylight. I am forged from all this romantic

   need. To feel in solitude. A boy builds his bridge across a
pyre. Something lodged beneath the heavy flames *explodes.*

   Frightened cars are acrid, carbon black, *lost.* To this day he
talks of purpose, reclamation, even though there never was.

An Opaque History of My Life's Work

I

Always in the summer, queen bee. The bent willow hunching by the crib. First light dulled to a point in the cool, tapped water. A rounded ocean. The Goats milk yellow at the teat as shadows of snapped grass are limbic beneath slow bodies. *Slow arc*, the stinger kisses the skin like a sword. *Lift me up, mother. Is this not true love?* There is acid all over us, flooding.

II

An opening of the smallest lilacs, *the buddleia*. A lobster claw reaching outwards into air, unfolds. Tubed serviette, let us hold innocence momentarily, the pink petals of a rose. In the fingers of a child the sun is pinched, tentative as a yolk. *Albumen. Chalaza.* There is wholesomeness. This woven silk sipped like custard feeds the body as it carefully grows its cup of cress.

III

Gradual copper sulphate. Its crystals suck the string between teeth. Attach gravely in secret. An accumulation of charge until lightning strikes a tree, nails itself to its own limbs. The cows in the field give up their boiled tongues and roll them off the chopping block. *There is a hacking of a hogs head.* A child sits on the floor, wide eyed, thinning. The colour is cobalt. *Is this not true love, copper blue?*

IV

It's a simple stillness. An afternoon watching sunlight track through glass. Such public confessionals prompt slake-less thirsts. *Ceylon tea.* One eye ideating, the other a walnut drowning in its own cream. Packed away inside a powder filled ball I light a fuse made from my own hair. It is thirty years long. All physical things are intact, although there is nothing left to see now. Nothing left at all.

V

When we have all exploded outwards, it is quiet. Projectiles in an eight pm sky. The planes in the distance seem to be stargazing. Red lights. White. Some disappear. There is something about the heart and time. About calmness. *Dear Brachycardia, dear sleeping dog*, space is just infinity at arm's length. I implore you, for death is coming. Lost child you are reaching inside yourself, little explorer.

VI

My life's work is dedicated to fluorescence, to keeping still. On occasion I'll sweep shrapnel for smelting. Pour it into sword shapes sweet with a metallic ring. *Sweet stinger, nasty little bee*, I can feel your six legs crawling in my ear. Peace is so *retrograde*. If I meet you, I hope you tell me all the things you know, like the best side for sleeping. That heaven is just a herd of horses baying at the northern lights.

Ellipsoid / Circumferent

The arctic is breaking, Canada.
There are bears on their haunches
looking to the northernmost curve.

I am up here looking down.
Wooden doll. Wool between bones.
Amongst plutonian Whale songs.

There is a calling and maybe God
will throw this burning sword to
the ground. To send flame, ash.

That this has to happen. Or unravel
strange shape. Breaking a mirror is
the shrillest at altitude. A sickness.

And wild eyes are a black kind of
black. I cannot settle anywhere other
than a graphite outline, a pencil tip.

A tsunami can be swallowed by the
sketching of the seabed. And harbour
mouths are mine to rescind. To build.

Weekday Octopoda Sad

For angular wind instruments
singing through low pressure.

Of blown glass sat underneath
ragged blanket, what shapes to

behold? what sounds? Subtlest
snake wrapped around its own

brittle tail, vertebrae crumpled
to a fist or *compression accordion.*

Whereby slip into odd drop of
rain, as colourant, snow under

microscope. *Be fractal.* Peering
outside, the hyacinths hold torn

packets. Free to fill & skipping
over every blackened slug back.

Shining of tar. *Elope* meaning to
evict these nominal childhoods.

Our dreams with every known
exoticism firmly crushed under-

foot. Facilitation is to dote on *all*
extremities; open heart removal.

Excavate the cavities, let arteries
tentacle out. *All hail king Octopus.*

Deep haemoglobin rich. Sew me
up inside a man so I can *manifest*.

As escapee. Deeply boundaried
with a love for life, not this ship-

wreck of dresser beneath an idle
trad house splashed all ruby red.

Paint marks; leeched bronze lung.
A headache soft as velvet pillow.

Rain now forecast for seven days.
Sit beside it with your work ethic.

Equestrian Civility

Death dispensed as conversant antidote.
Unrelenting hurricane eye-wall conjured
in the swollen fist of everything corporeal.
Scapegoat all feelings remotely, by sheet.
Get political. Become occluded, the body as
warm meat. The mantle splits open for us
to throw ourselves into. The shrill music
of our platitudes is this torn flesh of Earth.
Deep in the muscle bed, lightning strikes.
Cumulonimbus stacked up like pancakes
ready to stuff into throats. Minutes taken,
long division, *gag reflex.* Oily sand building
from the bottom of the feet. Spoons of fish
are *incredulous.* What remains to keep us
underwater stuck face to face with hollow
eyed spectres of our ludicrous selves, prune
skinned, herrings in mouth. To dream of
warm seas free of plastic, floating in the sun.
This interconnectivity. Things never seen; the
moons of Neptune side by side in the surf.
The blunted head of Tarpon, a suicide of
Barracuda. *Galatea, Triton, Halimede.* Things
exists inside and out, are very gently held.
Nothing matters. Not final breaths or business
acquisitions, think tanks or equestrian civility.
The last remaining rhinoceros. Just the magic of
missing the point. This wholly godless life
expressed in the pillars of creation, its gold,
lucent greens. Emancipation cloaked in dust.

Incision Claimant

Every jabbed sternum to
halt the opening of vessels.
    Ancient tooth witchcraft.
Observe the heavy wrench
    of loose jaw procedure.

Take them from the beasts.
Bear, Wolf, Archaeopteryx.
    Under mortar is a wetness.
Dentine; pulp in pestle ground
    to a paste. Chest preparation,

    or adorned magick licking
skin from ceremonial brush.
    A stillness. An alignment of
feral stars pulled under head-
    dress, mouth lifted up from

    splitting seams. Sometimes,
escapees in the form of flames.
    Bright arrow drawn from bow,
shot from mouth to heart. Under
    weight of wing, quench the

    phoenix fleeing into outer
space. Ice spheres away from
    suns touch, gas giants, sheet
of Saturn's ring. In times of need
    use each gnarled fist full of

molar. Bring all four incisors
to be crushed; freshly rooted,
bloody and tentacled. *Linger
archaic spell.* Better to empty
gums of all phosphate than

it is to eat wholesome foods.
Lunar magician technique to
dampen down each synapse
disguised as feeling. In lieu of
teeth, start removing fingers.

Beautifully Coloured Taiwanese Film

all my life, I have believed…if I mind my own business, no one would pay attention to me
— Rob Jabbaz

It's easier to sleep than it is to photograph the world. Wring out the sun, its saturates. Bleed meadowsweet into brackish water on the backs of rolling carp. They tell me everything about stillness; about grace. About the gap between life on the first floor and death on the second; between work and watching life grow and blossom in a whitish pink. Burst star. Burst Magnolia. Violence, which is freedom: a bright appley red warmed under lighting. The effervescent sop of soaking in all the places never knowingly seen. I take another picture, hide myself within its greyscale acetate, hide behind the absent tints to float again above the scented cotton of an uncomfortable bed. Someday, something will have to give. Some things will have to be put away. Some things unfinished, half written in ink by a horse bristle brush.

Lamplight, Lay Down Your Arms

Bodies are asleep. Mine is observant, wrung out
by a curtain crack. I pass myself through a sieve.

Nakedness eclipsed, partial; pectoral muscles, arc
of bloat. There is nothing whole here. Some spoilt

red petals, stamen attached as epaulette. Sown soil
prodded by wanton bursts, luminant colourations.

Malicious maybe. Maybe desire as fruitless exercise
bar the creation of something sacred. Stems left to

wilt conditions inconducive & bent frigid beneath
footfalls of a ghost who walks the line. *Sempiternal.*

Trapped by design of fragile creation. How heavy
the guilt of sex, of pleasure bent around a hazelnut

tree. A stork hung by a branch sings '*Do Not Want*'
– the raw contents of a cut throat. Old meat lashed

around a wire frame as pallid, palimpsest of youth.
As small slice of light sat neatly across a chest, held

momentarily in the cool air wrapped around thighs,
around shoulders. In awful elasticity, *I touch my side.*

Starvation pleads fake equivalence; of jubilant lust.
To eat. An ugly shape knows just how *good* it feels.

Midwinter Prayer Cycle

I've never needed to see the sun
more than this. Hanging in its tree.

    Waxy beneath fingertips groping for
    warmth. A three-millimetre gap between

winning & losing *everything*. The wind rises.
Herds of cattle, their muscular backs move

nervously. This space is too small for me to
    turn around in, to *breathe*. My powder

    falls like pollen, fills a room repurposed
for kidnap, for torture. I'm unsure why we

can't *all* do the things we love, but at least the
sky is beautiful. It is only bereaved at night.

    Yet still, I brush it against my wings.
    Emerging to a light that holds within

    its pocket the distance of our souls.
Of humid summers whispering that *twilight is*

rigged. To wake from sleep so clearly that it can
be touched. A peeling orange unravelled as I fall

    in & out of sadness. The hope of being born
    again. Renewed wholly, in the year of the pig.

I Am Coming to an End

I

Egregious war upon the self, I cannot escape these words. The cognisance of space between blades. The nascence growing green. Its repellence on licking lips, a yellow tongue. Of romanticism, hatred. Sickly horse, sickly shell holes, there is something here about shattering completely. Loud bangs in the field, its banners, torn flags. *Spill the yield of your hanging cloud*. In the space between opposing magnets is the fight. Five years. Thirty years. Forty. Looking backwards is *so sickly sweet*. Thirsty rag meets fuel meets the weight of yuletide loneliness. Tracer fire, tank tracks. A thankfulness for love but not knowing it. Ringing cheeks, a slapped face. Young convergent mouth, *'breathing into empty space is a deceitful cloak'*. A dagger stabs the wrong back; the body begins to grow. The past haunts its future yet to come along.

II

Attack worlds, attack continents. An attack helicopter is a windmill held between palms, set down smoking on the ground. Sugars sticky bridge from mount to mount. Bear arms, mother. Odd father, strategize trajectories - everything will be mutually assured. Take me to the streets. Lead me between the buildings ready to fall. Stand at opposite ends like *The Manchineel* and let them fly out from you. Black sparrows, magpies, a cormorant piercing the water like morning ice. I push these messengers into my skin. Hold them thick as tar, a midnight road. Sometimes war is a set table, a conversation over breakfast. A drawn sword hidden in the throat can be kept there for a lifetime until the smallest cut washes away skin and bone to the tributaries of the sea. To gather there its paltry foam, the swirling scum. Glance at resting bullets on the bed. At violence, at absence.

III

How to split atoms. On the skin the imprint of incisors, a molar.
From within, a blossoming of lilac shaken at the stick. Great admiral,
fanning peacock. The elegant cabbage white singeing against the
sun. A ghost beneath frosted glass, from behind the eyes. Take this
love and drown it in the blood boiling from the lips of the loveless.
Radiate incessantly. Make half-life a myth. Become as lethal as
an elephant's foot let loose above the kindling, weak dry sticks. A
father's fear purpling as the elderberries picked too soon. Dry bitter
wine swelling in a small stomach. Wrangle, detach, sublimate. Crawl
from your own mouth to live behind a ceiling looking down on all
your past pornographies. Smouldering electrical fire. Concussion
derivative. Grout yourself into the tiles of your own non-existence.
Avoidant corner house, mothers and children cross the street.
Fleetingly, a jet, a skeletal heat. Many, many missiles.

IV

Slide slowly out of yourself. There may or may not be colours. Old receipts crumpled and faded blow gently in the breeze of a blue room. Inhabit all four corners. This is death as a painters palette wet with oils, acrylics. Incandescent moon on a shelf smiles back. *Hold me in your hands, place me up there in the blackness and I'll light up, lemon meringue.* The moon winks. This is death, the night stands perfectly still. My body is empty and hung up on a metal hanger. I am the words sat behind a face that doesn't yet know how to talk. There are summer curtains waiting to be drawn, August coolness. I have no hands to hold up what luminosity has become; a pearl, a beating swan held by the legs. Bone chip. The rugged tip of the Carpathians creaking at the first clap of powdered icing on its peaks. I always said that something would have to give. This is death, and death says *'I want to live'*

V

Give me a voice tuned to major scales. Bright, augmented. Breathe new breath. Sit with a spider at dawn, drink the dew of his web. There is a quick collecting of things. Of foil and earth. Of generous helpings all sucked up. Vines twisted into shape like roots, slapped with fresh clay. New forms. Uncorrupted soil rubbed between thumbs inhaled. The cockpits are full of shadow. The streets bloom fresh flowers, fresh heads. It is said that *I am coming to an end*. Rebirth is a lollipop, malic acid, a reformation of sorts. The way litter is dragged upwards in a vortex. A fox cub in the early morn. I notice my new skin. It is delicate. Cough out this low-laying fog only for it to rise up, white dove, white owl. This thin sweetness is making me grind my teeth and the right words are scarce. Let it soar slowly, fantastic anti-climax. I put the plate back in the sky and wait for him to glow.

Equinox Combat Practice

An invitation, this modest breath. To a throbbing sun forming questions into words, an ear full of flies, *Calliphora Vomitoria*, humming as the waking up of things stirs the senses. Sucks on refuse. Slips in like a bad tongue licking at the roadside liquid neatly bottled and discarded, *a vile tangerine.* My inquiry is an apple in the air coaxing sharpened beaks. A coatless, cloudless existence. How is it *that all of this can be* when the shell of a motherless lamb is hidden by last year's helianthus now gone to seed. *Beauty.* Beautiful ignorant bliss. Sad snowdrop. The narcissi; slices of fresh lemon tart. The ruminants are chewing, laying still, somnambulant. In a field, the crying gull, a pointed rook amongst the rocks. The season is shrugging off its skin, *so allow the apple trees to blossom, slow bumblebee.* If I can't be changed, then plough me into furrows. Burst me open jelly bug. Flavour me obscene as August strawberries yet to dream of swelling.

September, by the Horse Pens

No one but
abnormal heat
asks who dies
first, *you, or
your heart.*

The summer
choked on its
own flies;
an absence of
lightning.

Abandoned
webs sagged
full of seed.
Brittle necks
snapped

by an old
man whistling
through the
shelf of his
incisor eroded

by the bit; old
songs, hard
winters. Wasps
desperate for
sugar, as am I

Blue Moon Theory

Break through your
   silken chrysalis to
leverage long limbs.
   Lift up the jawless

crown, a straw tongue.
   Gauge vibration
in the filaments before
   pausing perennially

as flat as folded ferns.
   Feel the thickness
of paper, the page.
   Reveal the wetness

of your colour, unroll
   prismatic peacock
tails. For when you look
   you'll see this place is

never the same as it
   always was, and
you're a different shade
   of *red coloured red*.

Prevalent winds pollen-
   thick amongst pink
petals. A sign that you
   are very nearly dead.

A city holds many
    flowers, such nascent
lushness. You can fly
    and everything is

tearing at the wingtips.
    You won't live long.
The moon redefined as
    a frozen figure eight.

III

Poems for Ursidae

I

grizzly winter coat contingent
roaming the *baited*
traps   nuzzling   enjoys
snow   wonders about energy
expenditure
trees conscious of
each and every leaf
pressed beneath
weight

II

claw rumination
to debate caring   or killing
how to hold bodies   *the young*
some scar minimisation techniques or
complex avoidant
        of being bear-like
                absorbent soil   its dewy
                                thick moss

III

halloween caught in
claw of tree   snout
pressed against window
bear-breath condensation ritual
accentuates every shade of ivy
as oubliette for slow
choking

IV

you are a cold cave
to crawl into
cold wall of winter dreaming of
rubied scalps   salted pelt
oval pearls of fat plucked from the
adipose   yellow eyeballs for
each salmon left to rot
beneath totemic Alaskan shadow

V

alone on tundra   charcoaled onto
horizon spirt level   searching ice melt
cavities   lunging   for ghosts of apples
fresh fruit   candlelit table to
crush   and *spill*   crack the bevelled
grains of oak   clatter sumptuous feast
to   sub-zero   valley   floor

VI

fantasy alpha fight swinging curved
weapons across all hateful faces
animosity bulked up like a fire mountain
explode from vents arcing blood across
snow   and the roars   the beautiful deep
roars that never happen

VII

sit on haunch to watch stratiform cloud
layered as grey carcass of
Narwhal   sit small and cowed
look up to measure
densities of grey as factual
comparison to happiness and when it
comes to pass   as does
bloated moon in
polar night

VIII

calendarise   deep   sleep
scratch out seven months   overeat
view cardiovascular systems   with
contempt   overwrought endocrine
schema   search rest   search
rehabilitation   wait for spring sun
the warmth of a cub   waking to see it rise

IX

Training schedule tentative for
mistakes   often bad tempered   often
contrasted   with views of mountaintops
projected upwards   sit upon stump
to ruminate   to splash in sacred
spawning grounds   I am there with
you   ~~(not there)~~   feel the ache of
metal lodged sidewards   I was your
size once   I remember

X

twenty five years isn't a long
time to string out linearity pause
existence wait quietly for storms to
pass from crooked mouth of cave
one day every known star in the
northern skies will cease to exist
and time will stop you become the
glistening on an endless rock face
no one will stop to wonder what
you are seeping into

XI

arctic silence as enjoyable cloak
a gnawing of the sea   the creak of blue
teeth   the arguments of moon
and sun   how to sit within it all when
the body is busied
the next meal
the next partitioned slumber
the next broken shelf sliding outwards
into nothing to really stand on.

XII

how beautiful you are
so small in
half-light trepidation
silhouettes observant of
us both
to be cognisant of
unseen serrations
frozen spears
mirror of water
shadows *shaped as bear*

XIII

I know you are with me
I am not with myself so
cohabitation dependant   symbiosis of
mercury dragged towards magnetic
north   there is no new language here
only a communion of foxes   the nearest
flowers opening are hundreds of
miles south you would look nice with
flowers in your hair

XIV

not unexpected   soundless shapes at
distance   echoing dance of torn flesh
cinematic   *not bear*   something born
from end ceremony   sent to test souls
recapture   *reborn* into blue light
does nothing   to accentuate the beading
of opened muscle bed   the violence
of finales   always waiting to happen

XV

negative coagulation test sits as
scattered jewels
it's funny   *the silence*
the beauty of river rock   the tongues
of earth so hard fought against   and
now I am flaking with all the gold
glinting in the slack water   *so elemental*
                               so galaxian

XVI

all that's left imprinted in sand
wettened   washed away
to stay here
by the banks of the *chilkoot*
holding moon in mouth these apologies
in the crater of Copernicus   love is
everywhere   the revenant footprints
of an injured mammal

IV

Of Evolution, of Apple Trees

It is remarkable how closely the history of the apple tree is connected with that of man
— Henry David Thoreau

I'm dreaming of you again. I made two handfuls of domestic weapons, *razor blades*, *pilnie-winks*. When you pulled back the covers they were pinched between my index fingers and two bent thumbs I've never sucked.

Before I closed my eyes, I watched a sow eat her young. Saw the movements of her face without guilt. Yet, in the drift yours neither droops nor lifts just remains wrinkled; *old violent hog*.

Lamplit dreams, spoilt dreams in a jar, the remnants of last year's jam. Wasp wings around crystals, cracked sugary skin. Clearly, *I am changed*. You lift up my eyelids, lips smacked on the rottenest of windfall apples.

They are leaden.

I am a tall tree, sound asleep.

Gore

Hair triggered conversations hard
    pressed against temple. Of late

night voyeurism convened in secret.
    Bathed in curdled light, the body

sags, red wine spills from its goblet.
    Cracked glass lifts towards lips to

gulp from a tannin lake. A thirst for
    pearlescent fat, muscle bed beading

and glossed with its guilt. Such disgust
    left to swing above what is sought so

curiously. Shameless bare bulb, wire
    ready for undressing by a notched

blade. Undeniable tool appropriated,
    selected with intent, *gives colour;* reds

blues, a rough wrought iron. The wet
    brown earth to be covered in, opened

up by hand. Fingernails caked, bloody
    in low decline *due south* of heaven.

A burial place for the undead. Midnight
    rituals executed in plain sight and

steeped in its bedrock. Mortar between
    suburban bricks seep liquid, clarity

dripping from a scaley tap. *Gathers*, in the
    the plastic valley of a rectangular bath.

To scrape up its matted hair, a murdered
    night lathered, scalded from the day's

cold skin. *They are trapped in there.* The box
    lets loose its butterflies, its sumptuous

grey ash. To cover those deep in loss, and
    strangled. Raw knuckles, less requested

numbness. So impressed upon, beneath a
    winter blanket dragged across its blood.

Swung sword, sharp cracks to the skull.
    Someone's heart extinguished by a cruel

candle cap. The only desire is to reveal from
    the inside out, to flood from the depths.

Disgrace then *my love*, is a grimacing jaw.
    All I ever wanted was to learn *how to feel*.

Consequence of Daylight

Astigmatised white eyeball,
forgotten, rootless in its case.
Unable to see the outline of

my body when I walk, or the
outline of my soul. It follows
silhouetted, *odd marble sphere.*

Gathering up the remnants of
shod skin. Dismissive yester-
years skilfully caught upon its

viscid tunic. Pirouette of dust
clinging to a lens once lifted
in-between finger and thumb.

Remembering to slot back in-
to raw sockets. *Familiar gritty-.*
ness as talking point. How to

spoil the scenery of sublime
spectacularism. Or at least an
erasure of unkind questions.

Such deeply thickened feeling
left within its rounded blister.
To roll, to glisten so aqueously.

Significant Repetition Analyst

The way to measure lengths of a shadow
is to return every night to the same place.

Lampshade to alcove. Rail to crawlspace.
An inflection point. The curving backs of

silverfish wriggling beneath the edges of
a cloyed carpet. If the truth be told, I'm *so*

boring to me. A grave estimation appears
leaden, cupped late in the clapping hands.

A thrown-up mercury cook-apple ready-
ing for precious metal assessment. Curl of

grey wave has followed me here. I won't
look it in the eyes. I don't bother searching

for atrocities, war crimes. Nothing changes.
Just a brittleness of nostalgia between teeth.

Second Shadow Competition

To climb up a hill so *Serpentine,* and then
    to find it. Above the sky held hostage with

wires across its neck. Simple whistle of song a
    train pulled early into dusk, and tortured by

vastness, a pastel palette. Upwards from the
    tail with heart in hand, a fear of hardening,

the firmness of a rosehip. 'Till at its peak, wind
    pacing four- legged, the tilt of a broken-

necked bird, *tumultuous.* A reddening tongue,
    a dewy red lip. Resting to feel the tightening

rope drag away summer's auburn worthlessness.
    Knowing not of love but asking to feel it.

Forgetting what it was, *the purpose,* but plentiful
    fields. Of bites abrupt, pink with lusciousness.

It's This Body That's the Problem

Everyone is telling me that I have to shrink   to disentangle
Sharpen words like *detach*.   Observe an olive ripen

Shrivel up like a lip   If you spill it all out onto fresh tarmac
let them kick themselves through it   I've spoken

too much about things   and its tired   Obvious as
ash glistening under wet weather   A black shape is

lagging behind   *Odd dog*   *Long ingrowing toenail*   The
questions are eating the answers in the fields   There is

something about the word *emergent* that conjures up visions of
crawling through tunnels   clambering up a herniated

spine   Pushes outwards into the flat opening of a vent
Asinine air!   *Oh torrid claustrophobia*   As the world

goes around and around   I must remember to get my clothes
ready   I must trim away all of this yellowing fat

Consequential Ways to Change Yourself

I

Curl yourself into the lantern of a wasp. Sing songs about knives, common hymns as salvation. Unenlightened, crawl outwards onto the back of an apple. *Some chewing. A clicking.*

II

Engage in unexpected conversation; Cannibalism, the undead. Nineteen seventies exploitation cinema as a vehicle for distinct personal change. Pedestrianised requirement, *intestinal realism.*

III

Structured swimming sessions. Embrace chlorination to dissolve mind / body partitions. Handcuffed at the blue slope, feel the warm water rush in. Antelopes rolled by a crocodile.

IV

Track macronutrients. Attempt to love the body. Hold devices to your skin so completely powerless between every known witching hour. Creep from cauldrons, snack like a young cub.

V

Talk about the colour of clothes; shape and depth. Analyse shade related perpetual imagery. Man beats woman, woman fights child, child beats them both to death with ball lightning.

VI

Nature as the terrible mother you always had. Spend time in inconsolable forest fires. Pull away meat from the back of a sad animal. Hemlock longs in the throat, orange sunsets are ironic.

VII

Craft programmes to embroider a flag with deities. Fly it above the cracked beams of your forever home. Meaningful crystals fill up the attic space. Garnet coagulant; amethyst birthstones.

VIII

To be completely open, install a zipper from sternum to pubis. Sex falls out, as do the genitals, as does the heart. Grind the remnants on a millstone, a broken horse with no steel shoes.

IX

Ask for help as often as required. Most relevant internet sites give a 15% discount of your first lonely coffin. Sizing facilities on-site are always available (but for Platinum customers only)

X

Help others forge keys from foraged metal. Distribute with complimentary mythical creatures. A sublimated Gorgon; Quetzalcoatl giving sword demonstrations for scared villagers.

XI

Implement reward sequences. Fifty-minute pain threshold, a coupon to the *all you can eat* buffet. Gorge, sequester. Fill a wardrobe with everyday inaction, some calorific night-terrors.

XII

Let physics settle on your tongue like snow. Absorbent, a cold transparency. Surrender to the stomach folding in its cavity or an emergency exit at the expense of never-ending nothingness.

XIII

Self-care; a selection of pine scented soaps. Exfoliant approach reminiscent of the poltergeist 'bathroom scene'; pull off your own face. Poke your fat down a plughole under hot spotlights.

XIV

Paranormal to YouTube algorithm ratios. Substitute humour for orbs, a face in a window. Abandoned hospital, heavy sinks. Write scripts, politely whisper into new recording equipment.

XV

Crucial time with your family. Look them in the eyes and have them repeat, you're going to die you're going to die you're going to die you're going to die, you're going, you go, go *you!*

Evolute / Become Perennial

Window bricked parapet
soaked in demilune substrates.
Mutes the night silk, a young
seed spun from scant prison

windows, lifts up the privet
where perverse secrets curse the
silhouettes running hairy legged
down the path.

To thirst beside ivory skeletons
of our favourite dead nuclear
animals. Jabbed, *right in the neck
of it.* Razor clam, hollow water.

A bird body, comfy *lived-in* ribs.
Polaris targets young backs only
when space knowledge sends us
spiraling into glossy sleep.

Grow stems. Slither up all *earth
wormy.* Chokehold tidy gardens
with unprecedented nighttime
surprise attacks.

This Room Is a Silvering

It looks to me

then slowly

turns

away   warm air   groaned

and barely freshening

whilst in

the mirror

I see myself

again

the *event horizon*

a table topped

with curves

pinched at   waist height

that I'm *compelled*   to watch   to wet with

iodine

before naked

skin is

set upon

take away   the genitals

the pink piggishness

pluck out

every strand

weaponize this

smoothness

unlearn sentience

on massive scales

a fireball   or *recipes*

for crispy pork crackling

analyses   of pen lines

tells all   that I am not

a surgeon

I never learnt

how to love

my own shape

but I can

paint it

with the best

of vantablacks   *old Octopus ink*

whilst all the teachers fuck

themselves   inside the bathroom

a body

will laminate itself

is this a memoir?

it makes sense   maybe

physical assault   a burnt

circle

circular

crow coloured

my body   *in verbatim*

because love

                    imitates life

                              the worst art
                                                   is made
          from arbitrary numbers

                    room eight eighty   eight

second floor
                    is just a room   *apocalypse now*
Martin
          Sheen

               maybe this is
                                   me   learning to love

          myself
                                                       again

   as shattered glass   reveals

                                        the weeping face
of David
               a broken spear
                              snapped
                                        just beneath
                    his
                         sculptured   feet

V

Transformation Cynic as Genre

What is it to change anyway
    the world is ruinous we
inherit bloat our firm upended
    bodies bulge from rounded
tins all rusted yesteryear relics

    Oil of innards worked via
circular hand to cloth lolling
    dry tongues cobwebbed
from light promoting health or
    healing or God its writhing

eight tentacled legs wrapped
    around throats head clamped
in a vice unsure about surgery
    or eye removal spoon it out
relentless twenty-four-hour

    positivity gag reflex this time
exists in a day as do its minutes
    maybe work more open wider
for tooth grimaced fission devices
    to be massively exploded into

I'm so very grateful to be alive
    you should too I see it clearly as
rimy glass from temporary home
    removal is where the heart is
all spiritually necessary *of course.*

Swarming Phase

Cantantopidae / or the way a cloud / breathes out its blackness / murmurates / around a singular locust / who questions / the nature / of our relentless scouring / of fields too irreparably scarred / the clambering of bodies / the gnawing of leaves and fruit / the existential comedy / of arable land / knowing only too well / its own thirst / and conversing with swarms / a gregaria of shape and sound / this clicking of wings / the question of requirement / for biblical scale catastrophes / *how dramatic!* / this evolution / or maybe we should call it / what it is / *mob rule* / the rush to mimic / such extreme ends / or wallow in God's wrath / the weight of knowing / that our ability to shapeshift / is nothing / but the split atoms / of stuttered apprehension / the false inevitability / of natural disasters

Imposition (death to ill omens)

Get in touch, lonely body.
Is there blossom? A bud?
This is pulling us apart, soft loaf,
so lost and out of reach.

Drab clouds snagged upon the stress
positions of cream whipped ceilings.
Self-surgery. Anaesthesia.
Nothing can be properly gripped.

Dismiss the encouragement.
To be a boat not the surface of the
sea gathering up its broken bits.
Once upon a time, pine chest, you

were ready to be filled. This drifting
between horizon and hallowed earth.
For nothing, strict appetite. Tentative
feet brush anemones, are knotted.

Thoughtless as a floating feather.
That bastard wings are necessary for
the beating. Launch upwards. Find a
way home, *young Albatross.*

In the End, the Soul Falls From a Limp Body

absolution as
corrupt concept

or complete
misunderstanding

of electricity its
wiring from

ground to sky once
deemed unquenchable

now manifest as
backwards falling

accepted wastefulness
in the irony of

cyclical birth or *rebirth*
samsara as exercise

how it might feel
the sensation

the guilt of *worrying*
about sensation

or gunshot accuracy
the clarification

that it has all been
for nothing

or *everything*
all at once

as endings rooted
in the mind or

ingratitudes of
a failing body

we have learnt
about linearity

our time
stretched out

like a severed
tongue thrown

into empty
laps

a black dog
shrivelled and limp

a swabbing of skin
the orangey brown brush

strokes of antiseptic
prior to first incision

Schedule for Steady Diet

Medium is a loaded word select
memories at random specifically
such worn uncomfortable clothes
misshapen ripe for neglect observe
every distant year ignored kicked
down the road folded inside bread
poked into dough eaten swallowed
you feel accelerations towards your
own end worried of course but there
is tomorrow to start over look her in
the eyes take a blood oath she suffers
so much at such a young age *she trusts
you* this isn't helping so recite the
words hold her stare feel her warm
kisses land like plump apples on the
wretched orchard grass break this
promise at your peril even though
encrusted space calls you upwards
such beautiful clusters of dust and gas
never seen before in such detail take
your plate fill it with nourishing fruit
some good old *soul food* hack open
that watermelon the one you've been
craving all these terribly hot nights.

Presentee Debate

Relearn how to play. To clean milk teeth
twice for health. Crack the shell of a star

above your head & let its innards engulf
you completely. Know it will char fleshy

coverings. You can become again, more
powerfully than splinters or a near miss.

It's travelling quickly towards us all, hell
bent on stretching out its vociferous cloak.

For resplendent tenderness. To cover skin
in vampire bats, velveteen wings. Fear not

patagium. The world takes back its blood
eventually. Fly towards it all, open ended.

Comfortable Room, Some Talking.

Loudness collects in places waiting to be opened. A slow breathing, like loam loosened around toes, buried feet. The anticipation of chrysanthemums opening in the sky that rise up like a cruel hand. The colours are beautiful. The way a palm squeaks the skin of a balloon as inside all the things waiting to escape are brought to the boil. I flinch. *I am flinching.* A naivety to voices froths from a bottle, froths over my legs. They are all so loud. Their noise is a dead body on a lawn. The heightening of greenness throttling the neck, the head, a sudden clapping of hands. Every year I light more fireworks just to stare at silhouettes. I tell myself that *delay is just fear of the unexpected* and so I hold them in my eyes, feel the angled grass beneath my soles. The thump of sound rising up and down again. From the ground across the cold sky or a cupboard door suddenly wrenched open to stark shouting. I remove my hands from my ears. Someone talks about rest. *Someone* is talking about rest.

Controlled Explosions

Mania as expressed
avoidant late payment
charges or the way

attic beams sporting
wounds dampen, are
always ready at night

to fall, suffocate like
duvets full of terribly
graphic dreams where

swilling weedkiller,
sweet sugar in mouths
ready for the rasp of

struck matches before
boom everything has
been controlled, is fine

until torrid water drips,
red lights on the dash.
Then know that I am

held into jarred position
besides bleak suits, very
tall expressionless men.

Dissect Recurrent Theme

Dawn raid on the withered finds nothing but
    dried straw. Boxed apples, limp bodies in heat.
Illusionary except for fruit flies landing on the
    centre of the soul; accentuated decomposition.

Walking away as central persuasion, the core of
    its almond scented seeds. Acetic cyanide rhythm
whitening the edges of a paring knife run along
    loved-ones lips. Every nomenclature laid to rest.

Deliberate infection unforgives our daily bread.
    Its broken pieces, densest crumbs; submergent
hearts in lieu of death. Precious unit. Sacrosanct
    family. My crust of self is soured; too bitter to

taste, the same as first disgust felt in recollection.
    Its lies of flavour. Lame horse limping to trough
cankered from birth magnanimous to avoid the
    breaker's whipping crop. Gelding trains gelding.

Rider trains rider. Man trains man to gulp down
    dander. Poisonous birds, their blood orange eyes.
Grown beaks to peck the sides of hands looming
    love. Occasional migration to the southern-most

reaches. Cleans feathers, tears off strips. Flesh of
    sun, dissect plump peaches. A citrine strength to
sustain dry fruit for our young to share, nourish
    lean growing bones. Sworn into this; *for this.* To

think of change as the simplicity of swords held
    in hammer grips. Parry fear, gouge out the rot
that lingers in the born marrow. To fall onto its
    sharpened point. Open up wound to pour out

dead rivers. The same stink. The putrid smell of
    every conjured disappearance. Maybe I should,
and change *nothing*. Draw upwards all swing-
    ing fists. From memory, coffin lids; cheap wood.

If this is knowing, then I am lost. Martyred to the
    grind of satellites signifying day to night, human
fuel for abnormal heat. This will stop. We will *all*
    stop. I've ignored my reasoning, my seasonality.

Made it thin. Sallow yellow fat; some waxy paper.
    Between twilight monstrosities find the flight of
a tawny owl, serene stillness, faded pine inhaled.
    Cold inwards breath, grow entwined in midnight

wintering practice. Orchard reclaims resin, sticky
    buds. Rose pink, apple blossom. That we pause a
while, untouched. Sleeping through enslavement.
    That I will become a shape for us, without shame.

My Own Ceremonial Killing

Which way is home, Capricorn? Cloven
hooves snag on black blankets. Nothing
but a murder cloud of liminal lights can
flicker. Celestial figures arctangent to an
orbit, fly away, bleed out brachycardic

hearts, *our open wounds for reconcile.* Lung-
less air emboldens acquiesced mountains
shrinking in secret, as blizzards augment
nectareous decline. The *big-bangs* colossal
coal furnace as ever-consumable hatred.

Nets tangled up in, lacerate, strip away
tides & colour from the sea. Oh fleeting
orange fox, arrow seeks flank. Prods its
steel to whisper gentle death into warm
ears. Friction holds the flesh tensile upon

entry. The muscle, *the muntjac* torn away.
Knowing cradle of grass that holds crown
above head for absentee mothers. Coveted.
Longed for. Talk is poison dripping intra-
venously, death looks on. Blue veins cool

the lumen, covets glutton appetite. Skeletal
weight defiant & set to fall. *Transmute.* Time
is no epigraph to save our souls, but exact
strategies to demolish *every building prior to
extinction level events.* Such advice is never

meant to be pre-medicated. How *not* to exude
denial? The existence of foals trembling in the
fog fields. Deep loneliness. Malnourishment.
Slid between bone walls, our *cruellest* months.
Of April's obstinate refusal, to cast off its days.

Future Cities

decouple submissive rage quotas
drag *haboob* / howled via wound
cleft / embattle scorched earth
shake every historical foundation
Apatheia retirement homes / abscond
this rooted memory / kidnap *all*
fourth industrial revolutionaries / force
with absolute threat / transmute ceremonial
flesh / into tensile skeletons / become
animal / set feathers within wings / ignite
kerosene persuaded anti-tails / bright
torches / pennaceous vanes / let kindness
become / let love become / all euphoric
citadels / will rise / rapturous exhalation
the shape / of your embracing body

VI

Ten-Step Sleep Incantation Ritual

Awaken
within the
locked tomb of an
ageing vehicle. In the apple
tree sitting quietly, ineffective
glass hammers. *Condensate breath, O
widening eyes.* Tiny feet on sewn leather
to push against. Parietal rests upon
metal window pillar. Necessary
pain augments abandonment
paralysis. A mouth is a
hollow. The bones
of geese
rattle the
roadside
cats.
Time
swoons
in its
afternoon
irreverence.

Some nights
the lake is empty.
A dusk of gentle
sleep to drink,
to rest beneath
the fruit tree.
A drumbeat of
teardrops to help
fill up its yellow
water besides
which a cold
child is pinched into
grey crescent.

Forty five degree single bed slips into the mouth of it. Great white; black eyes. Late night Halloween, the clouds around its lungs, around the ivory plate peering its magnolia through the jars; formaldehyde snake, clenched spider. Black and white television shows the shark bite a man in half as he kicks against its listless plastic shell. The way the mattress tears between teeth is sliced apple flesh. I asked for this. There is no rest. In the deep, only lantern fish.

It
makes sounds
the body when struck,
same as how the floorboards
creak as you fight your way across
a violent room. When you climb into
bed with me, push crab apples inside
my throat you never see it gather with
the others, never see its growth above
the acid mulch pyramiding in my
stomach, never see the magpie
buzzing in its branches
waiting for this mad
season to
end.

Mid-
summer
substrate
of early
morning
raps its
knuckles on
the door.
A dog barks.
Wind shifts.
Horses in
the school
field see but
don't tell.
Wasps have
gathered
around the
fruit bowl
just below
the cornice.

Adolescent dreams of
courtrooms; judge and
jury. *Obfuscate expression.*
Galleries of tall
blank faced
men. Crab
suspended from
ceiling by a thread.
Rotation of rancid flesh,
meat in shell. The verdict
spores from a
shadow wound. Fog
around my legs
and tethered, by
the feet, the wrists.
A peruke, a gavel,
an electric chair.
My eyes free to
wander. *I never
thought electricity
would feel like this?*
My body
smells like
freshly
baked
apple
pie.

Every sterile room a bed, a desk, a chair the height
to prop feet. Every academic night defeated.
Sleep curtailed by cigarettes; the candy
apple red of taillights in the valley.
Talk of man not mother. Mirror
twists image. Lycanthrope
doused in moon fuel.
Everyone is asleep,
acclimatised,
alone.

I still wake up
with every dead parent.
Orchard coffin under honey
crisp. Harvest's poor yield sends
breach of wind; a finger scraping
through the wisp. Everything is
pruned, tied back, eviscerated.
How to stop the burgeoning
beneath size ten feet, the coy
clamouring of fresh shoots,
spears, swords. It's meant
to lead the adult mind to
places of change but all
there ever is, is repet-
ition, cheap medium
density fibreboard &
a dusting of ash.

For Lorca.
For the sleep
of red apples.
For the blue-
prints of our
own appalled
bodies, the faint
way markers to
crawl towards,
the endless
labyrinth of a
broken mirror.

Stay awake
next to
persistent
self for
sleep brings
fallen fruit.
The sound
of drums,
of misery.
Finger on
neck, a
jugular
full of
bullet ants.
Book under
bed reads
Poneratoxin,
its paper
made from
repurposed lanterns. I hold heart in
hand; pulp-like, acidic. Fear of finite
time, its wasted effort blown into the
deepest
slant of
every
ditch I've
ever dug.

VII

Black /Blue

Tell me how that manifests, she
asks. The pressure of riverbed
clay holding tight a thick sheet.
It is me, and I am it, I would say.
Describe this as a background
noise. Percussion. Triplets. First
beneath the mud, the other is
decay relinquishing it's dead
cells. Thirdly my own eyes
opened and watching from
above. One part shale to three
parts disgust. No desire. Perfectly
lustreless. A tarnished coin spun
up from the crown of a thumb
that continues to exist, and
without question, lays gently at
the silted bottom under the
bellies of spear toothed fish. The
world breathes out. The body
gives notice. A dove released
from the hands of the deep, or a
white orb. The exhalation of soil
and bone seeking out pearlescent
light or a bubbling up of old
leaves, old meat. *Dear discordant
tilt*. This axis of a twin Earth has
been adjusted to spin away. Blue
rolling ball. Black water to blue.
This blue sky, all blueish.

Space Marine

The restless youth called *they want their neon midnights back* some pixelations a cassette tape full of songs you might place inside a hinged mouth tomorrow or next year when in adulthood your lost adolescence *'in-bloom'* weeps to death inside the patches of white honeysuckle the nettle bed left to sting itself towards restless sleep we'd suck the sweetness from the flowers albeit the urine taste & somewhat buried in the coma the bookmark of all these twilight years a favourite shirt some *D&D* dragon took five washes to peel away in graduated disbelief so crawl inside the comics that kept you safe be rancorous & ready to appear again a fluorescent needle pierces clouds from ground to sky *magnesium lance* a fire to burn the sides of demons penetrate the warped and thickening skin a flag thrust into rocks of unexplored planets shows belief readies the crust *in part* for walking to cry out *forward battalion!*

Latitude: 56° 00' 0.00"N

I pick a hole in my heel, dig out
calloused skin. A moment frozen in
nothingness but the peel of exposed
nerves. I sink inside of it. Into an ill tide
of water sick with a foam, waves curled
like wanton arms. *I'm trying to change,*
Lord knows I'm trying, but the Lord
made the Octopus master of the deep.
Master of long tentacles, strong suckers.
Some bad luck tales of molluscs sinking
ships. In a night washed violet the
waves break as high as a thrashing
horse. Plastics. Blood lanterns on
sopping white. Discarded wire twisted
into hands that grab with a rottenness
that wraps around wrists. A listless
ramp angled upwards from the sea and
slanted towards town. Of dwellings, its
matchbox fires, the soundest of
ignorant slumbers. Sand beneath
fingers. Umber of the body crawling
sideways as a wounded crab. Battling
up and out of myself and sprung into
motionless day. Its cups, an open book,
a white rectangular packet.

My Father Was a Teacher /
I Am an Escapologist

From our souls, forge misfortune dialect.
Some self-sell supposition as finance for
grand houses. How to dodge inquisition
panels, exchange superfluous language.

Flagellate our own backs, bleed publicly
with good grace. *Thanks for the disdain, I'll
tighten it around my chest.* Placed between
work and present mood, productivity as

a blanket for deadly night, mouth of cave
ready to be fed. My body tattooed, tainted
shape imperfect for *Vicuña* pelt. My father
felt his hands tighten on the hierarchies of

lost appetites; *pro nuclear war.* Lost to the
land, his garnet jewels, svelte kale leaves all
gone to ground. To participate I stuff my
sides full of earthy tuber, ripened fig.

Face sewn on from fragments of every lit
fluorescent tube left flickering. I float, but
the margins of cities purr luminant drone.
Shapes of ghosts demand to be exorcised.

Unlit, in the Middle of the Sun

Walking into kitchens just to pause.
Draw fingers through ageing grease.

A marbled sugar-glaze surprised sour.
Its tang to stop the tracks of feet more

concerned with agreeable shoes, not
these repeat patterns. What is change

but the same light, the same scratch of
claws on hollowed stacks. Pest birds,

or pestilence, or *petulance*. My drama
school certificate opens up like a wing.

Nothing is looking for *someone* to blame
and I could just pop obscenely my old

leather knuckles. *Disappear*. Cradle my
child as a Father, a purple of Amethyst.

How to heal throats, hold heads. *Be held
evenly*, even. Every cracked egg of sleep

leaks its yolk onto my pillow. Each new
moon in turn, an operatic non-believer.

All Old Flesh Is Ceremony

In my first life, I kept the body of two dead snakes by a pillow. Formaldehyde; arachnid in a jar. The lake soaked inside a fitted sheet, is cooled. Acidity charged by a brittle moon so acquiescent in its off-white. Surrender then, to gaping bullet wounds. Hollow points punched pomegranate, opening like hyacinths on domestic display, wide-eyed. *This is youth.* The study of gastropods slowly slid down. Thorns as delicious secret. *Deliciously derived.*

A slow-motion horsetail, a silhouetted winter lake. Your immolation sits between its strands. *O* beautiful mahogany whip, *O* beautiful bridle, gallop through this surf of raging blood. Our first lives, a lie. Unsafe. Conveniently erased. Scrub skin tarred and feathered in the deathly cold. Feet corrupted on sharp shale; tusk of driftwood. Jawbone a spear thrown as the stench of midnight mass gnaws itself back to blue. The outlines of brackish whales are gagged in their beached persuasions.

To begin again. I am naked by a window opened for bright bodies. Every breeze from every lake smoothes itself beneath the door. For bone dry mud- beds to break the back. A pupfish, a sandpiper. Old testament to new. A glowing new born crying on the shoulders of pillows like a leaf. All songs from sleeping seeds are sown from old letters, wax seals torn, scratched in ink. Calls upon the down-trodden to rise back up again, *to sing*.

Emergent from depths, to gasp, pull deeply in its air; *all tomorrow's light*. To pluck a glossy red apple, crunch it, wipe clean the chin. Seek the beaten heart, crocodile clipped. Ready to sketch the twisted roots squirming from the 'Sea of Trees'. Perform peristalsis, an instant cardiopulmonary resuscitation. The carbon of devious graphs licking pyrographic paper. Thunder as distant flatline; *a skull punched fucker*.

Let sorrow blow all the way out. Ring in residual tinnitus gentle as andromeda's silk, where death holds the hands of stars born to the sound of bending ribs. *Phantasmagoria!* Glory be to anyone but God. My skeleton is thrashing in the acid bath, flesh risen up of shape and colour. Become nebulous. A stallion chomping at the frothing bit.

What If I Just Run Away?

*

Burst world, a festering world boiling in a pan. Lank pale tendrils, a pigs head looking blank. Milky cataracts, our fretful sun rises, the moon gnaws on its own grey forearm. Such fetish horror, to bake our daily bread.

*

Four walled measurement curse. A squirrel pelt *marmota monax* hung from rusted facias neck tied rapping on a work-day window. Immortal season beast or *bestiaries*. The repetition of real or imagined dead animals.

*

A severed past knotted in laces kicked off to browse footwear catalogues for old, tired feet. Bootlace snake venom pushed occasionally into thirsty veins as deliberate ignorance ingests pain-tolerant test papers.

*

Burning world, *starved* world struck on a tinderbox. Bespoke tailored suit, Prada shoes coughed from the lungs of a charred street carcass. Politicians shovel coal to shut mouths. Placate greed, handfeed tiny birds.

*

Polar-bear winter fuel club discussing variable ice thickness. To trust in human meat as reliable energy source. Gather your bitter snow-storm. Invade empty streets. Chew them up besides cold, lonely hearths.

*

Restless sheet music. Polyrhythmic artery congestion table. The daily rise and shine as pestilence. Our gratuity packages are to be squeezed of all marrow. All souls liquified into bone thin broth. Moth at night, aimless.

*

A fantasy prison break. *I won't forget your face as I fly.* Blue-throat migrations. A freedom deathless as a drying room wrapped in oil softened fabric. *Argan. Saponin. Olive.* Essential lavender perfumes.

*

The expected pain of separation. An unzipping of skin to climb into the body of a fox. *To become the hunted again.* We can *all* go if we disguise our home as a death crater, some beautifully faked identity documents.

*

The arc split open, and two by two return to land. Split waves to see a horseshoe crab, a seahorse. Return your blood to sand, flesh to soil, and spooky ritual. Run *very* far away. Omnipotent creature, become disassembly.

Reviving the Corpse of a Leopard

Sunday's thankless tasks; a bloodshot eye prised open with a spoon, *cheap blunt steel*. Blue light from devices best smashed with tempered metal are left to linger. Bodycam footage. Screams from a finger as it scrapes, pushed deep inside a socket. There is a glitching. No *new* news. Its anger rolls cloudy liquid down the scorched valley of a cheek. Never enough thought put in, never enough *things completed*. Dissect the word '*pathetically*'. Pathetic man, pathetic hang headed shadow. It's nice that you're here but these nesting dolls you painted squeal revenge. You skipped over it to address a tangled garden. To ponder how deep a trowel might be pushed in, *unencumbered*. What will it mean when shades of red stipple the fingers; *ripe strawberry, sour apple*. There is only one shape on the tree and the branches cover the bent stems of peonies like a witch. I am growing as tired as the thin yellow grass I never cut. In the same way my contribution to architecture remains some bone chipped edges, the kitchen's old cups. This is some maligned effort. *You*, laughing at the repetition of 'let's talk more' and *me*, designating my ending to the crunch of trod eggshells. Know that time wasted bleeds out like a runt pig stabbed in the back. Hope then, for good memories. Of parenting. Of divine intervention. Hope for sound career advice. Hope for a full and fortunate existence. Hope to consume all and everything in a fire so blisteringly hot that the world steps out of its own skin. To ride with the Valkyries beyond the Kármán line and into the bad mouth of a wolf; the broken son of Loki carved into flesh.

Mediating Extinction Level Event

Children dance around a maypole. Red ribbon to yellow,
a navy blue, the sky shrouded with all our collective relief
flown at half-mast. *It must be the end.* A herd of liquorice
horses in the liquid field. This nostalgia smells like summer
salad. The way she used to roll the ham next to the egg, some
slices of bleeding apple. I wish I could have loved myself the
way I loved you. *Abrasion remembrance list* played in-staccato.
The blood runs away from the fingers, the pick-axe says hello
to the head. Fontanelles steeled in militaristic drum stroke
rudiment pattern as fireworks jabbed into cracks of pavement
are unable to dissolve. All hollowed out and spent. So quietly
seasonless. I hear the membraned voices downstairs creeping
in the yellow light of two conversant ghosts. Silhouette of
lonely bear twisted into tailfeather of comet, worn as scarf.
How many times should I disappoint this earth. Loose smiles
for every botched expression held in hand. How could I never
hold *yours* It is ending and the sea is perfectly still. We set fire
to our clothes. All dead swans knock together like wood.

Ineffective Methods For Living

Celebrate death dying cerebral life

Night-time republics of velveteen burlesque –

Legs & jaws; drippy stingers.
Unsubstantiated damage is still damage.
Distinct crumble quotient. Between fingers cause of
death is added 'ad-addendum'
Extended blue sky, things sound so far away.
A repugnant voice whose words shake the branches,
pulp unraked leaves into nauseous musk.
To feel your microwaves yellow yolk, you need to
crystallise the phantom pains pressing in your
stomach. Form it into figures, creepy arms,
bedsheet petals, serrated lilies. An anticipation of
scythes left shining. Look down to see your
son, your daughter. See emergent face in-
blossom, as otherworldliness. The night's black
somnambulance crowning day. Disgrace these
unmoved absolutes. Wholly gracious tortures of
convoluted apple trees. Cut loose by heavens rusty
razor. Uncared for at scale. *Hail Satan. Hail bleak wound
ratios.* Rapid comfort transformation. Dawn stillness
pressed between a page before foamy trivialities
bubble back up into lucid daybreak.
Gently held; occluded bloody earth. *So novel!
Such verve!* Kneel before wife, hooded before child.
Colour runs into nothing, into everything I always
called home, yet unable to be reminded of.

End Ceremonies

Hearing at distance the midday lull downing its iron
tools. Opaque window opened to suck out our wasted

lives, same as each aeroplane destined to withstand its
repetition of place. How to never truly find *any* ending.

Engines below the voice, below a failed sun given in to
retreat. Each sequestered moon, its silvered dreams of

manifesting *Deimos*. We fight back our own outrageous
shapes. From reddened surface left for dead for whom

absolution can *never* be given. Not the gazing of navels
or a venomous snake eating through its own toughened

tail. The wire of known peripherals, jagged, overgrown
pathways. Apple of the Manchineel held as weapon, as

plump grenade. A fist pummelling the back of our own
heads to become decorative ivory chalice, fit for the fire-

place. Holding massacre candles lit in remembrance of
who or what we thought we once were. *Ask me to dance.*

Tripped steps in the dark time of radical misplacement.
Wanting to live freely, gathering tight these barbed coils.

Unconscious plan in defeat, two competing silhouettes
waltzing into neon midnight, synchronous, arm in arm.

As final ceremonies build, we are risen up onto feet, heels
cracked running through the horse fields to the drumbeat

of desperate souls, appetites wet for the quenching. Face
to face with our enemy in the silvering of eternal mirrors.

This is me, and I am you, and we are speared by Whale-
bones discarded on the beaches of bloodlust bad dreams.

Tentacle avoidant. The Kraken froths in the deep, wanton
for a fresh torso to constrict. Where are the waking hours?

The arc of light warming skin, loving comfort of a mother.
Loving outline of a father to step inside. Such nostalgia for

toothache, for gnawed fingertips needling a sharp inward
breath. Without rage, entities are released from constraint.

Without constraint we are celestial. Soaring upwards, bird
of prey, plumage of stars. *Ask me to dance.* These epicentres

sit within the orchard, the wilding grass fed with the flesh
of fallen bodies. It is said that we will disappear, for all to

see the shape and sound of our mistakes. Build up to this
crescendo. Hold me tightly, for this is how it always ends.

Acknowledgements

Sincerest thanks to the editors of the following journals and magazines where some of the poetry in this book first appeared: *Ambit, Anthropocene, Atrium, Bath Magg, Berlin Lit, Blackbox Manifold, Full House Literary Journal, Ink Sweat & Tears, One Hand Clapping, Paradox Lit,* and *Poetry Wales.*

The poem 'Consequential Ways To Change Yourself' won the *Ambit Annual Poetry Competition 2022.*

Introductory epigraph taken from *The Great Sadness* by Federico García Lorca taken from *Suites (translated by Jerome Rothenberg)*

Beautifully Coloured Taiwanese Film contains a quote taken from the film, *The Sadness* (2021) written and directed by Rob Jabbaz

I'd also like to thank a whole host of individuals for their support and inspiration. Firstly, Aaron Kent & *Broken Sleep Books*, Emma Kennedy, Rue & Otis Kennedy, Charlie Baylis, Penelope Shuttle, Bobby Parker, Joe Kent, Wendy Allen for all of her feedback and friendship, Zoë Brigley, Alex Houen & Adam Piette, Claire Walker & Holly Magill, Rebecca Tamas, Dr Chris Laoutaris, JP Seabright, Leia Butler, Colin Bancroft & Nine Pens Press, Seanín Hughes, Alice Kinsella, Ian Patterson, Joe Carrick-Varty, Alan Humm, Matthew McDonald, Chloe Elliot, Dean Rhetoric, Jadyn Dewald, Anna Saunders, and Tom Snarsky.

Thank you to my wife Caroline and my daughter Dorrie.

LAY OUT YOUR UNREST